What Do You Do When ANGER Gets the Upper Hand?

JAY E. ADAMS

importance for our present discussion is the fact that words spoken out of anger (and that is what the context is talking about) must be directed toward destroying the problem, not toward destroying the person. Psychiatrists and others sometimes make the mistake of recommending pendulum thinking and acting. If someone has been holding in anger, they may recommend ventilating it toward others, toward a pillow symbolizing others, etc. But this is wrong biblically. It fails, because even though the energy is released in a new way, the new way is out of accord with God's Word and therefore just as wrong, as wasteful, and as counterproductive as the first. It is a matter of exchanging one sinful pattern for another. Moreover, you can see how this type of swing still leaves the problem untouched.

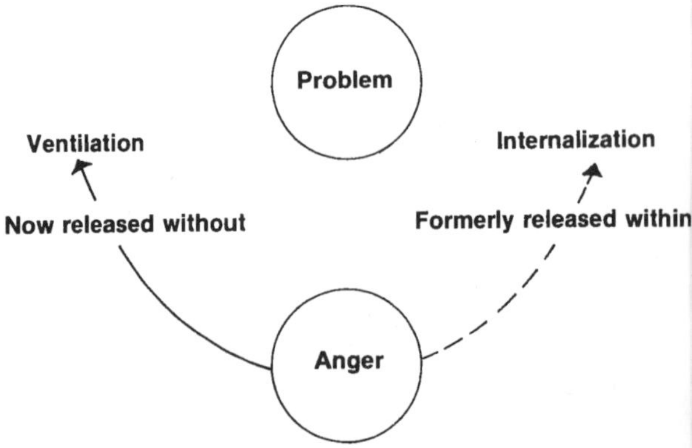

Or, in the reverse:

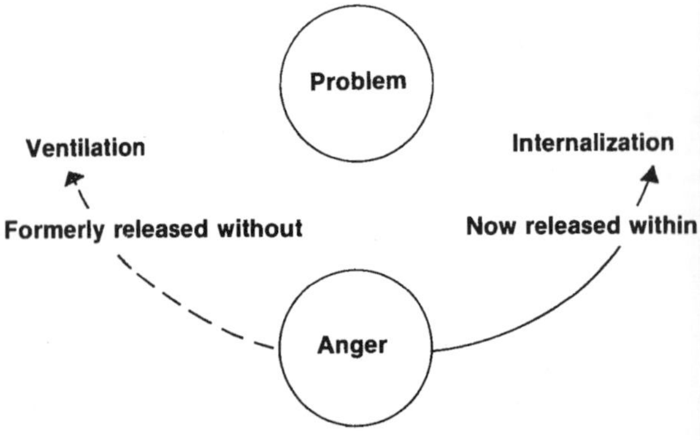

In pursuing either of these pendulum swings, as you arc from one extreme to the other, you move past the biblical middle and fail to release the energies mobilized by anger in a constructive way that will destroy the problem and strengthen the relationship one has with others and with God.

is a powerful motivating force that is intended to drive one to destroy something. But the difficulty is, God has not given us the right to destroy other people or to destroy our own bodies. Ventilation of anger is aimed at destroying others (or handy and symbolic objects around one). Internalization (unintentionally, but nevertheless surely) is aimed at destroying ourselves. Blowing up at people and things, as one vents his spleen, truly releases the energies of anger, but in ways that do not really solve the problem that occasioned the anger in the first place. Instead, these energies released out of control, and in ways calculated to hurt others, only do more damage. Clamming up, holding anger in, releases the energies of anger within one's body. These energies, intended to motivate one to do the right sorts of things to solve the problem that occasioned the anger, instead are misdirected toward one's own body and result in tension, colitis, ulcers, or other such miseries.

Diagrammatically, let me try to show you how these actions fail to achieve the purposes for which God put anger into man's emotional makeup.

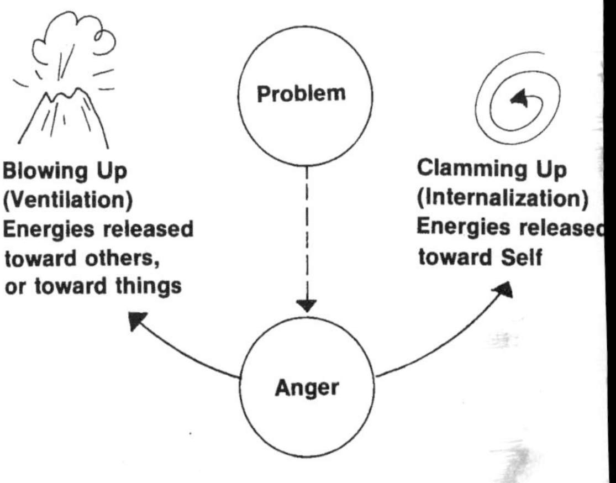

Notice how the energies mobilized by anger are misdirected. While in both instances they are released, these powerful energies fail to meet the problem. In contrast, listen to the important words of Ephesians 4:29:

> Let no unwholesome word proceed from your mouth, but only such a word as is good for building up, aimed at the problem that has arisen, that it may give help to those who hear [my own translation].

You see, our words to others—even when they have wronged us—must be words that build them up and that give them help; never words that destroy them. Such destruction of others is a prerogative that belongs not to us, but to God (read Romans 12:18–21). But of greater

"NO, I CAN'T CONTROL MY TEMPER!"

But you can.

"I can't."

Can.

"Can't."

Can.

"Then tell me how!"

Certainly—that's what I wanted you to ask in the first place. Like many others, you have bought the false line that under certain circumstances you are totally unable to control your temper. That is false, I say, because the Bible assures us that if you know Jesus Christ as your Savior, you can. God calls upon you to do just that: "A fool gives full vent to his anger, but the wise man, holding it back, quiets it" (Prov. 29:11).

"But that's just my problem; I *can't* hold it back and quiet it."

When you say *can't*, what you really mean is you *don't* or *won't*. You may have convinced yourself that you can't, but that doesn't change the facts. You can; God says so.

"Well, if you knew how hard it is for me to do so, I think that you might change your mind. You don't know how many times I have tried to hold it back, but in the end, I blow off anyway. You don't know the situation."

I think I do, and I still maintain that *can't* is the wrong word to describe the situation. Take Joan, for example. She complained that she lost her temper whenever she became exasperated with her children, and the frequency of those occasions was increasing. At times she blew off like Mt. Vesuvius. Ashes and sparks went everywhere. Well, Joan . . .

"I can identify with Joan!"

Good, I thought that you could, because when she came for counseling, she too said that she thought it was impossible to restrain her anger. She argued with me much the same way that you have. Then I said, "Joan, let me describe a typical situation, and then tell me if it fits. Suppose it is late in the afternoon on a rainy day when everything has gone wrong. You got your period today, the pot boiled over on the stove, your three preschoolers have been cooped up inside all day long, and . . . well, you fill in the additional details. Now, let us further suppose that the kids get into a scrap, complete with fistfights, whining, and all of the rest for the umpteenth time. You have tried, but this is it—you restrain your anger no longer. Instead, over some slight provocation, in a burst of volcanic activity, you erupt. Lava-like, words pour out. Fire and ash spout forth in all directions. Debris is everywhere. Kids are diving under tables, hiding in closets. It is a real spectacle. Now, in the midst of all of this, the phone rings. On the other end is Mrs. Green, head of the local gossip society. She is the very last person who you would want to hear you carrying on like this. So . . . what do you do? Well, you sweetly say to her, 'Oh, hello, Mrs. Green, it is so nice to hear from you,' etc. What have you done? Controlled your temper!" At this point Joan broke in: "That very thing happened just last week."

And you say, "It has happened to me too."

Well, then, you see, both Joan and you can control your temper when you really want to, when you are highly enough motivated to do so, and when you make a strong effort of the right sort. The problem is that you have learned not to bother to control your temper in certain circumstances with certain persons. But you have learned to control your temper in situations where you thought that you could not get away with such outbursts.

"I guess you are right."

This little vignette illustrates an all-too-common problem. Men and women—truly Christian men and women—*learn* to let go of their temper in the presence of members of the family, even though they have *learned* to control it before others. Husbands who give their wives severe tongue-lashings at least fortnightly become even-tempered sweetness and light personified at work and in dozens of social situations. The reason, of course, is that (as the italics indicate) they have *learned* to adapt their behavior to their situations. And, because this is a matter of learned behavior, there is hope for change. What has been learned can be unlearned, as a new, God-pleasing way of responding is relearned to take its place. Moreover, the fact that you have learned to control your temper in a situation of any kind shows that you can learn to do so. That means that you can learn to do so at home.

Isn't it strange, businessman, that you think it more important to control your temper with your boss than with your wife? "But I would lose my job if I lost my temper at work," you may protest. Exactly. You probably would. But you see, reasoning that way only shows how poorly you conceive of life's priorities. Because the money that you make at your job is a more tangible, immediate reality, you therefore give the job higher priority. Yet your relationship to your wife and to the Lord is a far higher priority. And you are damaging those relationships. Because God and your wife love you, you think that you can get away with abusing them both with your language. But you can't. Your fellowship with both is hindered. God has written: "Husbands, love your wives and do not be embittered against them" (Col. 3:19). Uncontrolled temper is never acceptable. It is sin. It is sin in the home as well as anywhere else. The fact that your wife puts up with you longer than your boss does not change the truth of that judgment. So, if it is sin, it must stop. And, as we have seen, it can be stopped. God Himself has said that He will help you to "put away all bitterness and wrath and anger and clamor" (Eph. 4:31).

"How? I have tried everything, but nothing has worked."

Well, it is clear that you have not tried *everything*; you have not tried God's way. It never fails. Before we get to the ways and means that are clearly set forth in the Bible of putting off sinful patterns of manifesting your anger, let us look at the other way in which many people sinfully handle their anger. Instead of blowing off, they clam up. They do a slow burn. They hold it in and allow it to pile up and to crystallize. They grow bitter and resentful, day after day rehearsing old grievances, licking old wounds. When the Bible speaks of holding back anger, it does not suggest clamming up and becoming resentful as the alternative. Holding back a sinful expression of anger differs from holding it in. Indeed, holding it in is the other sinful extreme which also is condemned by God: "Be angry, but do not sin; do not let the sun go down on your anger" (Eph. 4:26). The answer to loss of control of temper is not resentment, just as the answer to resentment can never be flying off the handle. The person who holds in his anger and stores it up sins just as surely as the one who does the Mt. Vesuvius.

"What then is the solution to the problem of sinful anger? On the one hand you say that the Bible condemns the ventilation of anger, but on the other hand you insist that anger must not be held in. Doesn't that leave us with only one conclusion—that it is always sinful to be angry at all?"

No, that is not the only way to go. While it is true that both of the manifestations of anger that we have talked about are condemned by the Bible, it does not follow that all anger is sinful. Indeed, in the passage just cited from Ephesians 4:26, notice that Paul says we must not sin *when we are angry* by clamming up and letting the sun go down on that anger. It is clear from the words, "be angry, but do not sin" that not all anger is sinful in and of itself. Anger, like every other emotion that God has given us, is a proper and useful emotion when it is expressed in a manner that is consistent with the principles of the Scriptures and used for the purposes that God has set forth in that Book. As a matter of fact, that anger may even reflect the anger of God Himself under such circumstances. Verses like Psalm 7:11 (God is "angry with the wicked every day") and Mark 3:5 (Jesus' "looking around at them with anger") give us a certain indication that there is such a thing as righteous anger.

Let us try to understand what is wrong with the two sorts of anger that God condemns and what is the biblical alternative to such manifestations of anger. First notice, neither one of the alternatives examined so far solves any problems. Both, instead, create new and worse ones. Anger

Now, in contrast to both of these schemes, let us look at the biblical alternative: aim all of your energies at solving the problem God's way.

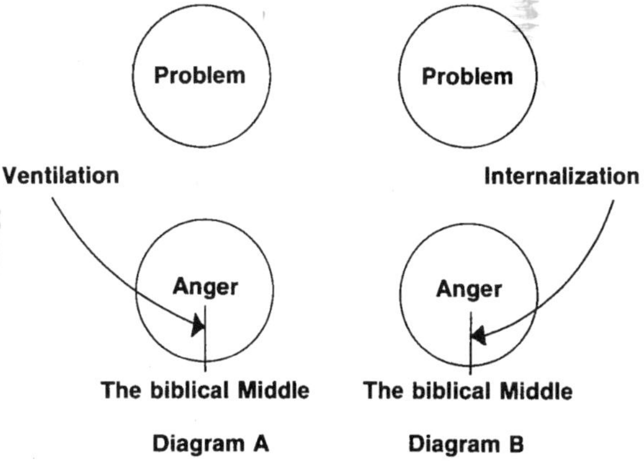

If your problem has been ventilation, outbursts of temper, blowing up (Diagram A), rather than swinging past the biblical middle over toward internalization, you must ask God to help you to hold back rather than hold in your anger. That is, you must learn how to release anger under control. If your problem has been internalization, holding anger in, clamming up (Diagram B), rather than swinging past the biblical middle over toward ventilation, you must ask God to help you release rather than hold in your anger. That is, you must learn how to release anger under control. When you do, the diagram will look something like this:

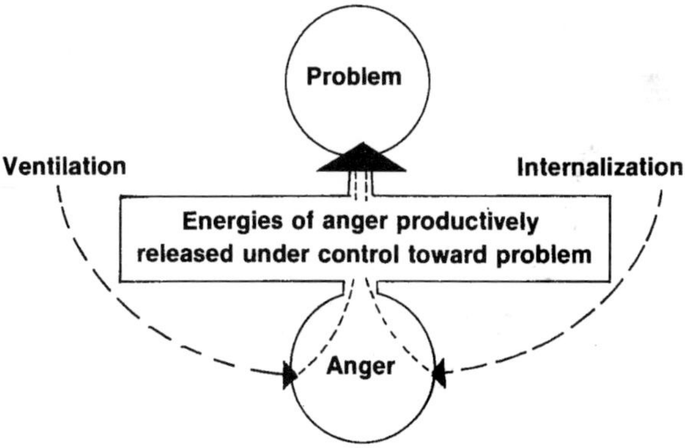

Only in this way can you gain control of this powerful and important force in your life. Anger, like a good horse, must be bridled. By His grace, God will help you to gain control of your anger so that you may use it for His honor if you try to follow the biblical directions about anger taught in these Scriptures. You do not have to make the change in your own strength, because as you prayerfully seek to follow the guidance of the Bible, the Spirit of God will enable you to do so. That you can depend upon if. . . .

"I thought that there must be a catch somewhere."

Yes, there is one, but only one. All this God promises to you IF YOU ARE A CHRISTIAN, but the promise is not yours if you are not. A Christian is someone who has learned that he is a sinner condemned before God because he has broken the laws of God. He has discovered that he cannot do anything about this himself, but he has come to see that God has done for him all that he could not do. Christ came to die in his place, taking the punishment for his sins. Thus, He has paid the penalty for the broken laws. Moreover, because God is sinless and because heaven is a perfectly holy place, Jesus has lived a perfect life in his stead. Just as all of his sin was taken upon Christ as his substitute, so all of the righteousness of Christ has been counted as his. And all of this took place when he understood this message and believed it (that is, put his dependence upon what Christ did for him in His death and resurrection). The very moment that he believed, his sins were forgiven and he was declared holy in the sight of God. That is what a Christian is.

Let me ask you, are *you* a Christian? If you are not, then let me urge you not to try to deal with the problem of anger first. Put first things first. Take a hard look at your life, recognize your sin (the anger is a good place to begin) and your need of a Savior. If God is showing you this, then trust Jesus right now.

Christian, while the basic dynamic for handling anger God's way has been spelled out for you, it is likely that you may need help in restructuring the particulars in your own situation. If so, seek the counsel of the person who gave this pamphlet to you, write to the contact point listed below, or read chapter 31 of *The Christian Counselor's Manual* by Jay E. Adams.

CHRISTIAN LIVING / COUNSELING
ISBN: 978-0-87552-044-5
EAN
9 780875 520445 50030

P&R PUBLISHING
www.prpbooks.com • 1-800-631-0094